This book is for:

_____

From:

_____

On:

_____

I hope your family's friendship with Jesus keeps
growing as you get to know him better.

Visit **MyLifetree.com/Kids** for more
fun, faith-building stuff for kids!

Notes From Jesus for Families
What Jesus Wants Your Family to Know

Visit our website: group.com

Credits
Author: Mikal Keefer
Editor: Charity Kauffman
Chief Creative Officer: Joani Schultz
Art Director: Michael Paustian
Lead Designer: Michael Paustian
Illustrator: Adam Armentano
Assistant Editor: Lyndsay Gerwing
PRINT ISBN 978-1-4707-7289-5
EPUB ISBN 978-1-4707-7290-1

Printed in China

001 China 0723
10 9 8 7 6 5 4 3 2 1

30 29 28 27 26 25 24 23

Names: Keefer, Mikal, 1954- author.
Title: Notes from Jesus for families : what Jesus wants your family to
know / by Mikal Keefer.
Description: Loveland : Lifetree is an imprint of Group Publishing, Inc.,
[2023] | Series: Notes from Jesus | Audience: Ages 4-10 | Summary:
"Notes From Jesus for Families is designed to help families grow closer
to Jesus, together. Written in first-person by Jesus himself, families
will come to understand how much Jesus loves their family. Jesus will
help them grow together, share, help one another, be kind, have good
attitudes, and invite Jesus into their family every day"-- Provided by
publisher.
Identifiers: LCCN 2023003416 (print) | LCCN 2023003417 (ebook) | ISBN
9781470772895 (print) | ISBN 9781470772901 (epub)
Subjects: LCSH: Jesus Christ--Teachings--Juvenile literature. |
Families--Religious life--Juvenile literature.
Classification: LCC BS2416 .K44 2023 (print) | LCC BS2416 (ebook) | DDC
232.9/54--dc23/eng/20230308
LC record available at https://lccn.loc.gov/2023003416
LC ebook record available at https://lccn.loc.gov/2023003417

Notes From JESUS for FAMILIES

What Jesus Wants Your Family to Know

by
Mikal Keefer

LIFETREE

Group

TABLE OF CONTENTS

Hello, Friends!

I love families—including yours! I love them so much that I chose to be born into a family when I came to earth. I know how to sweep, shop, and share with others—all the family stuff.

I want to be your friend—your best friend. But I also want to be a friend to your family.

I want to be part of your conversations. To pitch in when you need help. To laugh with you when you're having fun together.

So invite me to be with you all day, every day. I'll be there!

And here's something fun: I want you to be part of my family, too. For you to love and follow me, and for us to be forever friends.

Will you do that? Will you be part of my family, too?

This little book is filled with notes from me to your family. They're words I've said or helped my Bible friends write or say. They're words for you!

Jesus

i WANT YOU TO KNOW...

▶▶▶▶ I love you!

Friends show up for each other. In good times they're there with a high-five and *woo-hoo*!

In hard times they bring hugs and a strong shoulder to lean on. I'm that kind of friend—because I love you. Before you even knew me, I gave myself so we could be friends forever. I'll always love and watch out for you.

And I'm hoping your family members will be that kind of friend to each other. That how I love you is how you'll love each other. That when someone scores the winning goal, there are *woo-hoos* galore. And when someone loses a game, a bike, or a friend, you're there with a huddle of hugs.

Because you're not just family. You're friends, too.

Jesus

Let's become even better friends...
We love hanging out with our friends. We laugh with them, tell them our secrets, and help them. What would happen in your family if you treated each other the way you treat your friends? How would that look tomorrow?

"i am with with you always."

(MATTHEW 28:20)

Let's become even better friends...

Find a mirror and stand in front of it. Arrange yourselves as if you're posing for a family photo. Everyone smile, and be sure to leave room for me in the picture—we're family!

10

i WANT YOU TO KNOW...

We're in this together.

We're all in this together, you know. I want to be part of *your* family like I want you to be part of *mine*. And I want to do more than sit around watching you do all the work.

That's what your cat does. And I'm not your cat. I'm your best friend. I know families can fuss and fight. That not every family stays together. And sometimes things break in families that can't be fixed.

It hurts my heart, but I know it's true. And when those times come—when things are a little or a *lot* hard—I'm asking you to let me help. To hold on to me and hold on to each other, too.

Together, we'll get through what's hard. That's what friends do, you know. And we're more than friends—we're family.

Jesus

11

I WANT YOU TO KNOW...

You're important to me—all of you.

When I was on earth, lots of grown-ups thought they were more important than kids. Some grown-ups still act that way.

But not me.

I want to be friends with everyone in your family—no matter how old you are. That's because you're all special to me. And I've made you all special, too.

Maybe you're the little one in your family who draws beautiful rainbows. (I love rainbows!) Or you're a big kid who can do wheelies. (That looks fun!) Or you're a grown-up who fixes food for others. (Sometimes I made meals for my friends, too.)

You're never too young or too old to be my friend. Or to fit into just the right spot in your family!

Jesus

Let's become even better friends...
Talk about this: What's special about everyone in your family? Maybe it's something cool they can do, or how well they hug. Whatever it is, tell them about it. And then tell me. After all, I made them that way!

12

LISTEN... A LOT.

(FROM JAMES 1:19)

14

When you listen, you love.

People who know me are surprised at how much I listen.

I'm the Creator of the universe, you see. I know everything and everyone. It's not like people tell me things I don't already know.

But I love friendships, and listening is a great way to make and keep friends. It's a wonderful way to keep friends and family close and growing closer.

So do what I do: listen.

Listen when someone tells you about a good day at work or a bad day at school. About skateboarding like a pro or face-planting on the sidewalk.

Listening isn't just listening. It's loving, too.

Jesus

Let's become even better friends...

As a family, discuss what you're looking forward to. But don't talk—whisper instead. That way you'll all have to lean in and really listen!

i WANT YOU TO KNOW...

Be careful about judging each other.

It's easy to judge others. Maybe that's why it happens so often.
He didn't wash the dishes, so he's lazy. She broke a promise, so she's a liar.
Even in families, people are quick to judge others.

Often, too quick.

Maybe there's a good reason she couldn't keep her promise. Maybe he just
forgot about the dishes. Until you ask, you don't know. So before you
call people names or think you've figured them out, be sure you
understand them.

Even better, leave the judging to me. I know you better than
you know yourselves. And I can tell you this: None of you are
perfect. All of you make mistakes. And I'd give my life for each
of you.

So go slow with judging. And be very, very fast to love—like I am!

Jesus

16

17

HERE ON EARTH YOU WILL HAVE HARD TIMES. BUT TAKE HEART! I HAVE OVERCOME THE WORLD.

(FROM JOHN 16:33)

Let's become even better friends...

As a family, stand in a circle. Lean in, holding hands in the center so you don't fall. While you're leaning, say simple prayers for one another. I'll be listening!

18

i WANT YOU TO KNOW...

Life wasn't easy for my family, either.

Maybe hard things are happening in your family. Angry words. Lost jobs. Broken promises. Sickness that isn't getting better.

I know what hard times are like. When I was a baby, my family became refugees. We had to leave our home and escape to Egypt so soldiers couldn't find me. When I grew up, I once didn't eat for 40 days. And later, while my mother watched, I was hurt and left to die on a cross.

But with God's help, my family and I made it through every hard time. With my help, your family will make it through your hard times, too. I promise.

So lean on me. I'm here for you.

Jesus

i WANT YOU TO KNOW...

Even when you're busy, put our friendship first.

Quick: Count up things your family has to get done over the next week.

List all the big stuff: doctor appointments, soccer practice, karate lessons, and lawns to mow. Then add the little stuff, too: toenails to clip, teeth to brush, and bike tires to inflate.

Your family is busy!

No wonder I sometimes sort of drift out of your sight.

I understand. But remember, just one thing matters most in life, and that's loving and following me. That's what God's Kingdom is all about! When you put following me first, you and your family will have the patience to pull together and the peace that comes from resting in me.

Don't let being busy get in the way of what's most important—our friendship.

Jesus

SEEK GOD'S KINGDOM FIRST.

(FROM MATTHEW 6:33)

Let's become even better friends...
Write my name on a sticky note, and place it on the inside of the door leading out of your home. When you see it, think of me and remember: I'm going with you!

SPEAK THE TRUTH,
BUT DO SO IN
LOVE.

(FROM EPHESIANS 4:15)

22

i WANT YOU TO KNOW...

You can be honest *and* kind.

If there's a rule in your family to always tell the truth, that's great! But tell it in a loving way.

Let's say a few big drops of sauce dribbled from your burger onto your chin at lunch. You didn't notice, but everyone else in your family sees it.

It's one thing if someone whispers, "Time to wipe off your chin." It's another if that person points and yells, "Look, everyone! Tony has a sauce beard!"

Both statements are true, but only the first is also loving.

Telling the truth in a loving way makes truth easier for others to hear. It shows you want to be helpful, not hurtful. Plus, it shows that the next time you're wearing lunch leftovers on your chin, you want someone to let *you* know in a loving way!

Jesus

Let's become even better friends...

Balance a pencil or pen on one finger so it doesn't fall off. How well do you think you balance telling the truth with being loving? Do others in your family agree? Why or why not?

23

You won't always get what you want.

I have some good news and some even better news.

The good news: You can ask me anything. You can ask me for a snowstorm tonight so you don't have to take that test at school tomorrow. You can ask me for a job that pays lots more money. You can even ask for a pet monkey that'll do all your chores.

And the even better news: I'll probably say "no" to all of that. Especially the monkey.

You see, I want you to love and follow me, and anything that gets in the way isn't good for you. Like taking the easy way out on a test. And having so much money that money is all you think about.

With me, you may not always get what you want, but you'll always get what you need most: me.

Jesus

24

Let's become even better friends...
What are three things you'd request, for each of your family members? Talk about that as a family and then...ask. But no monkeys!

YOUR WILL BE DONE, NOT MINE.

(FROM MARK 14:36)

25

i WANT YOU TO KNOW...

It's good to be grateful.

Some of my friends are very good at wanting more.

A bigger television, a snazzier laptop, a longer lunch hour. I know they want these things because they tell me all about it.

But try being grateful for what you have—for what I've already given you. Pay attention to those things for a day, and see how it makes your life better.

Practice being grateful for things, for people, even for problems. They can all bring you closer to me if you let them. All those things can help you grow and keep growing in your love for each other and for me.

It's okay to ask me for things. That's fine—really. I want to hear what you want and need.

But be grateful, too. That's where you'll find happiness and joy.

Jesus

Let's become even better friends...
Tell your family what two things in your home are your favorites. Why did you pick those things? As a family, wrap up your talk by thanking me for all you have—and for each other.

26

EVEN ON HARD DAYS,

BE THANKFUL.

(FROM 1 THESSALONIANS 5:18)

27

"HEAVEN AND EARTH WILL DISAPPEAR, BUT MY WORDS WILL NEVER DISAPPEAR."

(MATTHEW 24:35)

28

i WANT YOU TO KNOW...

I keep my promises.

I keep my promises—always. And that includes my promises to your family.

If you know and love me, I promise to be with you. I promise nothing can separate you from my love. Not now, not ever.

I promise if you follow me now, it's worth it in the end. Worth it a bazillion times over.

I promise when you ask my forgiveness for a not-so-great choice, I'll forgive you. I don't hold grudges.

And I promise when it feels like nobody cares, I care. I care from here to the stars and back.

Because you and me—we're family. Now and forever.

Jesus

Let's become even better friends...
As a family, read these Bible verses about me and my promises: Deuteronomy 7:9; Romans 8:38-39; 1 John 1:9; 1 Peter 5:7.

31

i WANT YOU TO KNOW...

I'll help you adjust your attitudes.

I love you just as you are right now. All your warts, your wrinkles, and the silly things you do—none of them surprise me. And none of them make me love you less.

But I also love you enough to not let you stay just the way you are. I want you to grow in how you follow me like you're growing in other ways. I want to help you think like I think and care about what I care about.

It's called "transformation," and it starts with our friendship. The better you know me, the more like me you'll become.

So let's be even better friends tomorrow than we are today.
You'll be glad you did—and that makes me glad, too.

Jesus

Let's become even better friends...
Got a ruler and pencil, and mark your heights on a doorway.
How much do you think you'll grow in six months?
What will help your body grow? What will help you
grow in your friendship with me?

30

It's hard to share, but you'll be glad you did.

Sometimes there just aren't enough cookies to go around.

But even if you think you'll miss out on something you deserve, it's good to share in your family—for lots of reasons.

When you share, nobody feels left out. You make others happy. And sharing helps you be a bit more like me.

I've shared a *lot* with your family. I made you, brought you together, and gave myself so we can be friends now and forever. And I'm *still* sharing with you. I share things like sunshine and music and joy each and every day—because I love you.

Sharing is more than just splitting chocolate chip cookies. It's what love looks like.

Jesus

Let's become even better friends...
Find a cookie (or muffin, doughnut, or piece of buttered bread) and share it so everyone in your family gets a bite. What in your family do you find it hard to share? What, if anything, might make sharing easier?

"THE GENEROUS WILL PROSPER."

(PROVERBS 11:25)

33

¡ WANT YOU TO KNOW...

I love when you talk about me.

It feels great when your family brags about you, doesn't it?

"That's my sister singing—isn't she super?"

"My dad learned Spanish. Bueno!"

"My son is such a cool kid—I love him!"

It feels good when you brag about me, too. When you tell people who I am and how much you love me, you're helping them become my friends, too. When you talk about me in your family, you're reminded that, even if you can't see me, I'm with you.

Besides, I talk about you all the time. I'm always telling my Father you're special. That I love you. That we're family.

Because that's what we are.

Jesus

Let's become even better friends...
Use sticky notes (or paper and tape) to turn your refrigerator door into a Brag Board. Write or draw one reason you're proud of each family member, and post it for everyone to see. And remember to make notes about me, too!

34

i WANT YOU TO KNOW...

I love when you talk with me, too.

It makes my day when I hear from you. Some people call it praying!

I love it when you share your lives with me. I like to hear what's hard and easy for you, what you want and need.

But I also like when you listen to me. It goes both ways, you know: Friends talk *and* they listen. That's how they get to know one another better.

So here's an idea: How about if, *as a family*, you talk with me? That way you'll not only learn more about me but also learn more about each other, too.

Let's have a conversation. I can hardly wait!

Jesus

Let's become even better friends...
As a family, take turns answering this question:
What's something that made you laugh or cry this week?
When you're done sharing, just say, "Amen." I was listening, so it was actually a prayer!

37

i WANT YOU TO KNOW...

Sometimes families get messy.

Mary and Joseph were my parents when I lived on earth. When I was 12, Mary and Joseph took me to Jerusalem for the Passover Feast. You can read all about it in the Bible. Lots of people in my village went and then walked home together. Mary and Joseph thought I was in the crowd headed home, but I wasn't. I stayed behind.

Mary and Joseph searched for days before finding me. My mom said how worried they'd been. But I told her she should have known I'd be in the Temple, my Father's house.

It was a long, *long* walk home.

Maybe your family members sometimes misunderstand each other, too. When that happens—when things get messy—do what my mom did. Keep looking for ways to connect. Don't give up on each other.

Just like I never give up on you.

Jesus

Let's become even better friends...
Let's take a family walk together. As we walk, talk about these things: If you could go anywhere as a family, where would that be? What's a favorite family memory? What's a family memory you'd like to have?

YOUR FATHER AND I HAVE BEEN SEARCHING FOR YOU EVERYWHERE!

(FROM LUKE 2:48)

i WANT YOU TO KNOW...

You can give your worries to me.

Do you ever worry?

Of course you do. There are lots of bullies out there, lots of ways your plans can fall apart. So long as you can lose your keys, catch a cold, or forget to turn in your homework, you have a reason to worry.

Except—you don't.

When you worry—especially about the big stuff—remember I'm here to carry those worries for you. I'll always be with you, always love you, always be your forever friend. That makes those worries seem a little smaller, doesn't it?

So relax. Tell me what's going on. Instead of hanging on to your worries, hold tight to me instead.

Jesus

Let's become even better friends...

Write your worries on slips of paper, and place them in a Bible, tucked in next to Matthew 11:28. As a family, tell me about your worries and then let me get to work. In a week or so, pull out your worries and see how you feel about them then.

41

i WANT YOU TO KNOW...

Fighting doesn't turn out so well.

Why is it so easy to fight with family members?

Maybe because you get to pick your friends, but you don't get to pick your family. You're stuck with someone whose snoring always shakes you awake. Who uses your stuff without asking. Who doesn't flush when finished.

When you feel yourself itching for a fight, instead of yelling, take a deep breath and calmly ask a few questions.

"Can we talk?" "May I tell you how I feel about this?" "What can we both do to fix this problem?"

Invite me into those conversations. I'll remind you that—even when you're angry—you still love one another.

And I love you all.

Jesus

Let's become even better friends...

Here's family fighting that's actually fun: a thumb war tournament! Play until everyone has won and lost a match, and then talk about this: What can you do to make sure you fight less as a family? And how can I help you?

AVOIDING a FIGHT IS a GOOD THING. DON'T INSIST ON QUARRELING.

(FROM PROVERBS 20:3)

43

GENTLE **ANSWERS** ARE FAR BETTER THAN **HARSH** W**O**RDS.

(FROM PROVERBS 15:1)

11

i WANT YOU TO KNOW...

Your words matter.

Here are two words to know: *react* and *respond*.

You *react* when someone is mean to you and you answer without thinking. You *respond* when you think before you speak, choosing your words carefully.

Because your words matter—a lot. They make situations better or worse. They fire up arguments or settle them.

When people lied to me or ignored me or hurt me in the worst possible ways, I didn't react. I responded. I knew my words mattered—and so do yours.

If you need help controlling what you say to your family or friends, tell me. I'll ask the Holy Spirit to give you a hand.

And since I'm picking my words carefully, here are three words from me to you: I love you.

Jesus

Let's become even better friends...
Practice thinking about your words before you speak by having a conversation with your family. But before anyone talks, that person has to pause three seconds first. Let me know how it goes!

45

I WANT YOU TO KNOW...

It's good to appreciate one another.

It's easy to take your family for granted.

After all, they're always there. They're not like friends who'll go away if you ignore them. Your family *lives* with you—you can brush them aside, and they'll still show up for breakfast tomorrow.

But that's not what it means to be family.

In a family, you stay interested in each other. You show up for each other's school plays. You ask how life's going and listen to what's said.

We're family, and I pay careful attention to you. I love it when you do the same with me. And *you'll* love it when your family pays attention to one another.

Let's do life—together. It's better that way.

Jesus

Let's become even better friends...
Pick an evening and spend two hours together—screen free. Talk, listen, laugh, play a game, pray, do anything that lets you have fun as a family. See how it feels to really pay attention to one another...and me.

46

i WANT YOU TO KNOW...

I have a job for your family.

I want you to love each other the way I love you. And that's asking a lot.

It means being patient, even if you don't feel like it. And not being jealous when someone else wins the Scrabble game. And not being rude even if you just stubbed your toe.

It means treating others the way you like to be treated—even if others don't always do that for you.

And it means not giving up on each other. Or yourself.

That's how I love you. That's how I'll always love you.

Jesus

Let's become even better friends...

As a family, spend 17 minutes speed-cleaning your home. Sweep the kitchen, scrub the bathroom, wipe off the table—anything that helps you serve one another. Because serving each other is another way to love like I love.

"BE KIND TO EACH OTHER."

(EPHESIANS 4:32)

50

i WANT YOU TO KNOW...

You can choose to be kind.

Maybe you've heard it doesn't cost anything to be kind. Well, *that's* not true.

Being kind may cost half your candy bar. Comforting lonely friends costs time you could be playing video games. And hugging your aunt who smells like hair spray and soap can make your head spin.

But kindness is worth it. It makes your home a place you feel loved instead of just a place you live.

When you're kind, you pass along a little of the kindness I've shared with you.

So be kind to each other.

Jesus

Let's become even better friends...
As a family, decide how you can be kind to a neighbor without that neighbor knowing it's you. Then let's go on your sneaky mission of kindness—together!

i WANT YOU TO KNOW...

It's okay to get mad—if you do it the right way.

Maybe you've heard that I don't want you to get angry. That when you do, I'm disappointed in you.

Not true.

I know you sometimes get mad. I made you to feel lots of feelings, and anger is one of them. But when you get angry, do it the right way.

If you're angry with your family, tell them how you feel and why you're upset. Then listen carefully to what they have to say about the situation. You may find you've judged someone too quickly.

Invite me into that conversation, too. I'll help you make peace so you don't get stuck in anger, carrying grudges and being mean to one other. I'll help you fix *what* you can *as quickly* as you can. And you'll all get a better night's sleep!

Jesus

Let's become even better friends...
Set an alarm clock for sundown. When it rings, talk with anyone you're upset with. Talk things through, forgive each other, and see how much better tomorrow feels!

"**DON'T LET THE SUN GO DOWN WHILE YOU ARE STILL ANGRY.**"

(EPHESIANS 4:26)

53

i WANT YOU TO KNOW...

In families we forgive one another.

Friendships don't last long without forgiveness. And neither do families. Sooner or later, someone in your family will hurt your feelings. Break your stuff. Say something you don't like. It may be an accident—or be on purpose. They may feel sorry—or they may not care.

You'll have a choice. You can slam doors and hold a grudge. You can try to get even by hurting the person who hurt you.

Or you can forgive. You can tell what caused you pain and give that person another chance.

I know it's hard, but I'll help you. I'm good at forgiving others because I've had lots and lots of practice.

Like when I've forgiven you.

Jesus

FORGIVE OTHERS,

JUST AS GOD HAS FORGIVEN YOU.

(FROM EPHESIANS 4:32)

Let's become even better friends...

Forgiving and letting go takes practice. Have each person in your family pick up a piece of trash and drop it into a garbage can. How is that like forgiving and letting go? How is it different? As you talk together, I'll listen, too.

I WANT YOU TO KNOW...

You make great cheerleaders.

Some things are easier when you have help.

Like playing ping-pong. Splashing through a game of Marco Polo. Remembering to be loving and do good.

In your family, cheer when others love well and do good. Applaud when someone's kind to strangers. When someone comforts a friend. When someone helps a neighbor in need.

Join me in applauding, celebrating, even tooting a trumpet or two! When you're loving and do good for others because you love me, it's like you're doing good things for me. And you're helping others see how knowing me is changing you—for the better.

And remember, I cheer when you do good for others in your family, too!

Jesus
X

Let's become even better friends...
Pick one person in your family, and have everyone else spend 60 seconds doing good for that person: finishing part of a chore, giving a hug, saying encouraging things. Then do good for every other family member, too. Remember, when you do good for others, you're doing good for me, too!

HELP EACH OTHER BE LOVING AND DO GOOD.

(FROM HEBREWS 10:24)

57

You can trust me.

Think of someone you're close to who you trust—a lot. What has that person said or done that helps you trust them so much? Whatever it is, I'll bet you can say the same things about me.

Do you trust people who tell you the truth? That's me. People who understand and love you? That's me, too. Do you trust people who want what's best for you and stick with you? That's me from top to bottom.

I'm here and will never, ever leave you. Not now, not ever.

When you're afraid, I'll be right beside you. When you're sad or lonely, I'll stick close to you. I'm here, and I'm not going anywhere.
So trust me enough to stick close to me, too.

Jesus

Let's become even better friends...

Up for a little family stick-close practice? Have everyone lie flat on their backs on the floor so the tops of their heads touch. Take turns tossing Cheerios or M&M's up in the air to see if someone can catch them in their mouths. Then talk about this: How does sticking together help us as a family?

YOU CAN TRUST ME, SO STAY **CLOSE TO ME.**

—

(FROM NAHUM 1:7)

MORE NOTES FROM JESUS FOR YOUR FAMILY

You'll find lots of notes from me in the Bible. In fact, the whole Bible is one giant note, one way I tell you who I am, what I've done, and how I feel about you.

Here are a few special notes for your family to read...

WHEN YOU NEED PATIENCE

Luke 6:31
"Do to others as you would like them to do to you."

Ephesians 4:2
"Always be humble and gentle. Be patient with each other, making allowance for each other's faults because of your love."

Proverbs 15:18
"A hot-tempered person starts fights; a cool-tempered person stops them."

WHEN IT'S TIME TO FORGIVE

Matthew 6:14

"If you forgive those who sin against you, your heavenly Father will forgive you."

Matthew 18:21-22

"Then Peter came to him and asked, 'Lord, how often should I forgive someone who sins against me? Seven times?'
'No, not seven times,' Jesus replied, 'but seventy times seven!'"

WHEN YOU'RE LOOKING FOR JOY

Psalm 118:24

"This is the day the Lord has made. We will rejoice and be glad in it."

Romans 15:13

"I pray that God, the source of hope, will fill you completely with joy and peace because you trust in him. Then you will overflow with confident hope through the power of the Holy Spirit."

Psalm 92:4

"You thrill me, Lord, with all you have done for me! I sing for joy because of what you have done."

Philippians 4:4

"Always be full of joy in the Lord. I say it again—rejoice!"

WHEN YOU'RE LEANING ON ME

Proverbs 3:5-6

"Trust in the Lord with all your heart; do not depend on your own understanding. Seek his will in all you do, and he will show you which path to take."

John 15:5

"Yes, I am the vine; you are the branches. Those who remain in me, and I in them, will produce much fruit. For apart from me you can do nothing."

WHEN YOU WANT TO LOVE ONE ANOTHER

1 Corinthians 13:4-5

"Love is patient and kind. Love is not jealous or boastful or proud or rude. It does not demand its own way. It is not irritable, and it keeps no record of being wronged."

Romans 12:10

"Love each other with genuine affection, and take delight in honoring each other."

DRAW A FAMILY PORTRAIT—AND INCLUDE ME!

Remember, I'm always with you. I'm right beside you. I love you all.